IN NO PARTICULAR ORDER

Another book of poems by Fergal Barr

In No Particular Order

Another book of poems by Fergal Barr

Order this book online at www.trafford.com
or email orders@trafford.com

Most Trafford titles are also available at major online book retailers.

© Copyright 2020 Fergal Barr.
All rights reserved. No part of this publication may be reproduced, stored in a retrieval system, or transmitted, in any form or by any means, electronic, mechanical, photocopying, recording, or otherwise, without the written prior permission of the author.

Print information available on the last page.

ISBN: 978-1-6987-0204-9 (sc)
ISBN: 978-1-6987-0224-7 (e)

Because of the dynamic nature of the Internet, any web addresses or links contained in this book may have changed since publication and may no longer be valid. The views expressed in this work are solely those of the author and do not necessarily reflect the views of the publisher, and the publisher hereby disclaims any responsibility for them.

Trafford rev. 07/11/2020

 www.trafford.com

North America & international
toll-free: 1 888 232 4444 (USA & Canada)
fax: 812 355 4082

'A few words'

In 2011, I published my first book of poetry. A bit of an oddity really because had anyone predicted 10 years beforehand that I would have written poetry never mind publish a book of it, I might have looked at them funny. That old adage about strange things happening was never so true. Now, here I am, with a second book.

In the past when people have heard I published a book of poetry, some jokingly ask, 'bit of a poet are you?' to which I reply, 'bit of a joker are you?' Joking aside, I almost recoil when anyone suggests that I'm a poet. There are poets and then there are those who write a bit of poetry, at least in my humble opinion. I most definitely consider myself to be in the latter category.

I never wrote poetry at school, nor in college, and was never part of any poets society, dead or alive. I cannot recall where and when I started but I think I just put pen to paper one day, in response to a feeling or feelings triggered by what was probably in the great scheme of things, a non-event, but a few years down the line, boom, a poetry book was published.

Up until I published the first book (and beyond), I did continue to write and decided I would include these in a second book, never actually knowing if it would come to fruition. I would write sparingly, sometimes in response to things going on, maybe a series of words would come to mind and I'd jot them down, or I'd observe certain things and write about it. Obviously, the more poems you write the closer you are to the goal of a second book and in the end this has proven to be the case.

One of my traits is to make constant 'to-do lists' and to top it off set certain goals for a given period and then work on them through to completion. I don't like 'unfinished business' so to speak, preferring closure, and recently I revisited (during 'lockdown') what I had written, and had to make a decision - draw a line under what I had done or finish it? There was only one answer – get it off my to-do list.

However, I like things that make sense but I was 'stuck' with 65 poems. There was nothing very logical about publishing a book of 65 poems. I looked for some rationale - I'm 50 next year but I couldn't publish a book of 50 poems to celebrate, that point had already been surpassed, and I didn't want to entertain the prospect of a third book as I wanted to draw this chapter in my life to a close. It then dawned on me. Yes, I am indeed 50 next year but having been born in 1971, writing a further six poems to round it up nicely to said number would give me the reason to complete this book. Now that makes sense and so, I got my writing hat on and finished the book.

The book contains 71 poems of varying lengths and topics, some of which are obvious, and some not so obvious. I reckoned, if you are fortunate to still be around to mark such a milestone, i.e., 50th birthday, and wanted to mark it in some way there could be worse things than publishing a book of poetry. The book is entitled In No Particular Order, because well, essentially there is no order to it, not even chronological.

So that's it, the rationale behind the book. It just remains for me to thank all the people, things and places that provided inspiration for me in different ways, some funny, some frustrating, some reflective, some sad, and some heartbreakingly so.

An enormous shout out to Graphic Designer, Michael Robertson. Once again, and as always has been the case down the years, he can take my limited one-dimensional description and with his vivid imagination brings things to life.

Lastly, if you shelled out a few pennies to buy the book, and have made time to read it, Thank You!

Fergal Barr

In Memory of Elitsa

Yuli and Elitsa, A beautiful, beautiful couple
His adoration adorns her
Her care for him knows no bounds
Together they share an unconditional love

A beautiful, beautiful couple
He looks to her for inspiration
She looks to him for the love she craved
Together they are what love should look like

A beautiful, beautiful couple
He seeks of her reassurance
She smiles longingly at him and takes his hand
Together they are unrelenting

A beautiful, beautiful couple
He would want no other
She would have it no other way
Together they show us how it can be

A beautiful, beautiful couple
He thanks the stars for shining on him
She looks to the ground where their seeds are sewn
Together they remind us of what we could miss

A beautiful, beautiful couple
He knows he is loved
She knows only his love matters
Together they are more than it can be

A beautiful, beautiful couple
He could ask for no more
She knows that only with him there is more
Together they are what we believe it to be like

A beautiful, beautiful couple
He cannot imagine life without her
She knows what dreams to imagine
Together they are what dreams look like

A beautiful, beautiful couple
He is her heart
She is his soul
Together they are butterflies among us

A beautiful, beautiful couple
He looks up to her always
She looks over him eternally
Together they are with us....forever

IN NO PARTICULAR ORDER

In No Particular Order

Another book of poems by Fergal Barr

Contents

People it's not always necessary **9**
Remember **10**
Are we so desperate? **11**
Life's Important Questions **12**
And so it wasn't to be **13**
We're only human **14**
Let's call it Love Making **15**
Well Dressed Man **16**
Every Time **18**
She is Laura **19**
You know who you are **20**
Intimacy can be **21**
The Majestic Miss Looney **22**
Out of the blue **24**
What a world we live in **26**
I don't get it, I just don't get it **27**
Madiba **28**
Love is a very confusing thing **29**
When they've gone **30**
Some accidents **31**
The Sores on our landscape **32**
The Internal Angst **33**
I guess not **34**
Who is she? **35**
Garrett so Smarrett **36**
Have I ever……? **37**
If I was in love with you **38**
The Government **39**
Doesn't he remember? **40**
As if Lior was my light **41**
How can I…. **42**
The fisherman and the mermaid **43**
Pleasing Others - Part I **44**
A Portrait of Tina **45**
When I think about…..I remember **46**

Waiting **47**
I wanna live in a country **48**
It's much more than that **50**
I sit on the sidelines **51**
Who am I kidding? **52**
Austerity **53**
I don't need… **54**
What a Nation the UK is **55**
The Humble Politician **56**
The Starbucks User **57**
Three Hours from a Knock on Your Door **58**
On Reflection **59**
Failing Forwards **60**
Websites – the stuff of legends **61**
The Facebook User **62**
Heart Stopping **63**
Struggling **64**
Inisheer **65**
Galway **66**
A Single Heart **67**
Joe **68**
My Garden **69**
Picture Yourself **70**
Pleasing Others - Part II **71**
Saving Grace **72**
There's not a day **73**
Encore no more **74**
How do I say I Love You on this special day? **75**
I can't escape you **76**
Old Man **77**
Why do people do what they do? **78**
The place, it was a-jumping **79**
The Resignation Poem **80**
Sacked and Dumped in a week **81**
50 Years, 50 Lessons **82**

People it's not always necessary

Lads it's not always necessary to talk out loud to let us know you're here
Ladies it's not always necessary to stay in the outside lane because you can
Girls it's not always necessary to wear make-up & fake tan to be desired
Young people it's not always necessary to curse in the absence of your parents to prove
your independence

Parents it's not always necessary to resist imposing rules just coz you did shit when you were young
Kids it's not always necessary to grow up quicker than your body will allow
Lads it's not always necessary to wear your jeans half way down your arse because someone told you it's stylish
Men it's not always necessary to treat females in that way because you don't know otherwise

Parents it's not always necessary to project your insecurities onto your children because you lack belief
Girls it's not always necessary for you to show us your body for us to admire you
Men it's not always necessary to drink so much because you have the space for it
Leaders it's not always necessary to be up front to prove you can lead

People it's not always necessary to wear labels to make a statement
Men it's not always necessary to win in order to preserve your status
Lads it's not always necessary to cheat just to ensure you'll be remembered
Folks it's not always necessary to be ignorant just because you believe it's better to get them before
they get you

Bureaucracy it's not always necessary to create rules so we that follow
People it's not always necessary to create excuses because you fear honesty
Kids it's not always necessary to have it now because parents lack courage
Politicians it's not always necessary to toe the party line to appear relevant

Lads it's not always necessary to strike out because you can't find the words
People it's not always necessary to assume because you can't make time to reason
Ladies it's not always necessary to think ill of our intentions because experience has taught you so
Men it's not always necessary to step up because history has told you to do so

People it's not always necessary to be serious just to prove you care
Believers it's not always necessary to convince us because you need to save us
People it's not always necessary to create fear because you don't understand
Society it's not always necessary to crave just so you can be included

People it's not always necessary to resist so you can remain independent
People it's not always necessary to pretend so that reality doesn't take hold
People it's not always necessary to do something just to make yourself feel better
People it's just damn well not always necessary......

Another book of poems by Fergal Barr

Remember

Remember when you worked your ass off to make sure we got that holiday each year
Remember when you stared down the barrel of a gun to protect me
Remember when you gave up your Monday, Tuesday and Saturday nights for years to serve others
Remember when I 'dobbed' school and all you had to say was 'do you wanna waste school like I did'?

Remember when all Eilis had to say was 'wait till your father gets home'
Remember all the difficulties with letters, words and numbers but you still had the resolve to work all your life
Remember all the guys who never got of their ass but you succeeded in holding down two jobs
Remember how you would create strange and exotic places like 'Ballinaspluck'

Remember HOI 8723, CUI 1821 & LXI 5719 and your pride in maintaining them
Remember how every penny you had you earned through your own endeavour
Remember no matter how hard Friday Nights and Saturdays were you persisted
Remember when you used to say 'sure as long as you have your health'

Remember when there was a family crisis you were the one to step in
Remember when there was a problem at home you never thought twice about getting out of work
Remember how you built Derrybeg into Barr family folklore
Remember how you used to cycle with us out the 'back roads' on sunny days

Remember how you used to tolerate so many 'are we nearly there yets?'
Remember how you would do anything for peace
Remember how you used to forgive us no matter how challenging we were
Remember that look you used to give us and we'd just know to stop messing

Remember the faith & trust you put in us allowing us to do things normally reserved for others
Remember when we'd go to Derry City matches and we'd stand with our own peers
Remember when I made you a grandfather again and you welcomed Carol with an embrace
Remember how you creatively turned the radiator into a breakfast alarm call at the weekends

Remember how you would eternally believe no matter how many times people let you down
Remember how you always found a way to fix things even though you weren't a Tradesman
Remember the values of respect, patience, humility and forgiveness you instilled in us
Remember that you were this man and you still are this man

Are we so desperate?

Are we so desperate we don't even question?
Do we desire so much that we do not enquire?
Need we crave so long we fail to see?
Are we so needy we fail to ask?

Have we wanted so long we know not what to critique?
Did we yearn so hard we accept without reason?
Might we want to climb so high we covet only crumbs from the table?
Are the lights so bright we care not for their source?

Is there so little we've known that answers merely placate us?
Can we tolerate ambivalence because we fear the consequence?
Are we so crazy for success that we blind ourselves to reality?
Do we concern ourselves so much with kind words we fear language itself?

Have we accepted spin as the new discourse because we are deaf to the truth?
Should no bad word be uttered as it may deflect smiles of the many?
Do we just go on our way because to think might make us unwanted?
Dare we stand up and be counted or seek sanctuary in the disease of anonymity?

Do we seek only glory because our achievements have been so low?
Will we lessen our resolve because we fear being props in a ganda battle?
Shall our approach be one of three evils because we just might have to choose one otherwise?
Are we to be a pale shadow of ourselves just so as to guarantee sunlight?

Do we accept the written words of others because it is there in black and white?
Are we so minded to will victory that we lose our will to think?
Can we be so aloof to our conscience that our struggles no longer define us?
Must we sit on the fence because it is more comfortable than sitting on our laurels?

Will we demand no less than our fair share or merely huddle around our gracious prize?
Are we happy to remove the voices in our head in return for peace of mind?
Must we defend the indefensible so that we do not have to bear witness?
And do we just bob along because it's easier than treading water?

Are we really so desperate?

Life's Important Questions

What exactly is bothering you?
What are we assuming?
What aren't you telling me?
What are the things we need to deal with?

How am I presenting myself and my ideas?
Who is it I really need to engage in conversation with?
It's reality for you but is it actually reality?
What would it be like just to accept yourself as you are?

What are the things that have influenced my life – what has made me the person I am?
What are the current vacuums in life – what are the fundamental gaps?
What keeps you awake at night?
Every journey starts with a step but can you take the first one?

What do you need or not need to happen to make this work?
How do we get to the point that we don't ask questions that are structured around the reward of feeling in the right?
What will be the one area where you sustained your passion and creativity to make a difference?
What is presence and how do we get it?

Where do the deep, rich, profound feelings in life come from?
What recent events or ideas give you hope for the future?
Why have you framed the question this way?
Are we merely an extension of those who have lived before us?

And so it wasn't to be

And so it came to pass it was never meant to be
No end of hoping to close the story brought it any closer
And of course I always hoped for that moment when we'd meet and just sit down and talk
and draw a line under the past and move on without complaint

You see, I don't like unfinished business
The kind where's it's all left unsaid
Where we head in opposite directions without so much as a goodbye wave

You see, I always thought you'd come back some day
The dawn of realisation would hit you
That what we had was very special
Something eternal

But hey what the hell, it wasn't meant to be
Even that closing conversation
Just to set me free

It wasn't that I wanted to continue
Just so we were at peace
That we could pass each other without duress or having to cross the road

I hoped and hoped and almost prayed that a time might come to pass
That you realise that it's not worth it to hold onto the angst but to simply let it go
That someday a friendly conversation might bid us on our way

Another book of poems by Fergal Barr

We're only human

We're only human, we find people attractive so please don't be surprised if I ask you out
We're only human, we all need company so please don't be alarmed if I ask for yours
We're only human, we all need companionship so please don't condemn me if I seek yours
We're only human, we all need love so please don't snigger if I dream of yours

We're only human, we find smiles beautiful so please don't reject me if I tell you so
We're only human, we all need to feel wanted so please don't dismiss the idea that I might want you
We're only human, we all need to feel desired so please don't humiliate me if I tell you that you are
We're only human, we all have love to give so please don't be unnerved if I want to share it with you

We're only human, we all have lots of thoughts so please don't run if I tell you I think about you
We're only human, we all get emotional so please don't belittle me if I get emotional about you
We're only human, we all have feelings so please don't begin to ignore me because I feel for you
We're only human, we all have opinions so please don't judge me if I feel I can confide in you

We're only human, we all know attachment so please don't detach from us if I become attached to you
We're only human, we don't always get it right so please don't hate me if I don't get it right with you
We're only human, we all have to change so please don't go changing if I want to change for you
We're only human, we're all a little vulnerable inside so please don't look to the door if I reveal a little to you

We're only human, we all like to laugh so please don't shy away if I laugh a little too much with you
We're only human, we all want to grow old with someone so please don't scream inside if I thought it could be you
We're only human, we all like to socialise so please don't be afraid if I invite you for a drink
We're only human, we all need a little bit of attention so please don't be cynical if I show you some

We're only human, we all need to feel attractive so please don't be surprised if I still ask you out!

Let's call it Love Making

We nurture it, we maintain, we build it, we sustain it
We hold on to it, we drive it, we value it, we survive it
We belong to it, we enjoy it, we dream of it, we toy with it
We embed it, we strengthen it, we die for it, we lengthen it

We are tied to it, we possess it, we talk about it, we caress it
We make sure of it, we grip it, we taste it, we sip it
We wait for it, we long for it, we dance to it, we write the words to a song for it
We hold out for it, we believe in it, we cherish it, we would never deceive it

We arrange it, we transform it, we smooth it, we dare not ignore it
We cradle it, we tend to it, we flex for it, we even bend to it
We haggle for it, we succumb to it, we risk much for it, we even plumb new depths for it
We will fight for it, we will exist for it, we won't hide from it, we will persist for it

We stand guard for it, we defend it, we prolong it, we lend for it
We are hearty for it, we are grateful for it, we narrate the story to it, we are fateful because of it
We stand tall for it, we gather en masse for it, we unfurl our flags to it, we let no-one dare trash it
We will not compromise on it, we will persevere for it, we will embolden it, we will adhere to it

We find solace in it, we have consolation from it, we triumph by it, we ensure trepidation with it
We leave no stone unturned for it, we will not stand still with it, we build dreams from it, ambitions we will fulfil for it
We will fall for it, we will endure for it, we will dig deep for it, we will ensure resolve for it
We will buy time for it, we will forsake for it, we will live & breath by it, we will make love for it

Another book of poems by Fergal Barr

Well Dressed Man

Well dressed man, well turned out
Everyone must know, the message must be clear
Sunglasses wore whilst inside
He exudes cool, she is left in tow

He takes control but gentlemanly he is anything but
His frame designed by a commitment to his ego
His looks groomed so he can't entertain doubt
She is merely an ornament

Sitting across from one another body language dominates
Glimmers of hope in occasional smiles
Conversation is light but difference glows
She is in his slipstream

A feast arrives
One of his choosing of course
They indulge
Breaking only occasionally to exchange pleasantries

Time passes slowly as if the meal was their last
Emptiness spreads across their plate
Food for thought

Pause for reflection, mutterances barely audible
He flexes his vocabulary in tune with his posture
He invites her to partake in discussion

She has permission always
He sees to that
Almost reticent to respond unless antagonism is his game

She throws him a line, a means to an end
A carefully delivered recital
An effortless sortie into his triggers

He is unfazed, unmoved....undeniably at ease with the situation at his disposal
He knows she is riled
She knows that he knows she is

She reaches forth, her fingers in a gentle brush of his hand
Her attempts to engage him beyond his ego seems pointless
He epitomises modernity

A modernity that is aloof, that extols values out of step with care and compassion
Values in keeping with bravado
Values that do not lend itself to sentiment

No sentiment retained here
Treat 'em mean keep 'em keen approach seeps from his eyes
A contemptuous look designed to question her integrity

Why would she tolerate such measures?
Why does she need company of a walking bicep to feel loved?
Why would she compromise on truth, compassion and belief for a love built on testosterone?

If she does so he contemplates she deserves it
My will be unquestioned, my desires unchecked, my responsibilities unaccounted for
I am King, she is no queen, she barely makes princess

Her eyes, her hair, her looks, her needs are majestic
Her quest for love would seduce many a compassionate soul
An equal to her deliberations, her questions, her tears, her thoughts, she could easily have

She knows of course
She senses, she feels, she always did, she always does
But her benchmark set she cannot sacrifice perceived accomplishment, vanity reigns supreme

Stuck in a place almost of her own making
She determines her fate, equating it to her lot
Justifying no other fate would be so kind, a lucky hand she believes she has been dealt

He knows, she knows, he knows she knows, she knows he knows
They both know
But not a word uttered and no attention befalls same

How can she accept such a fate?
How can she continue in such a vein?
How can she contemplate a life without truth?
A future without that which she really covets, there is actually margin for error

Why would she honour such a conviction?
Why would she accept less than she is worthy of?
Why would she choose an ill-fated journey?
Why lie in the gutter but only glance at the stars?

Why oh why should she placate him, caress his ego, fulfil his notions of grandeur, reinforce
his mistaken beliefs, affirm his sense of ill-informed self?

Why? Why not?
She is human, she is no different to the rest of us
Our own fallacies collide with our values, our sense of worth equal to that which we can secure
Of course she'll stay, he needs a trophy, she needs to believe

Every Time

Every Taste, Every Smell
Every Touch, Every Yell

Every Feel, Every Caress
Every Yearn, Every Press

Every Pull, Every Push
Every Lick, Every Gush

Every Sense, Every Squeeze
Every Suck, Every Tease

Every Kiss, Every Time
Every Word, Every Mime

Every Finger, Every Sigh
Every Inch, Every Thigh

Every Breath, Every Moan
Every Moment, Every Groan

Every Wish, Every Trust
Every Part, Every Lust

Every Minute, Every Second
Every Style, Every Trend

Every Idea, Every Tear
Every Heartbeat, Every Fear

Every Now, Every Then
Every Time, Every Bend

Every Spank, Every Hand
Every Game, Every Demand

Every Passion, Every Glory
Every Opinion, Every Story

Every Journey, Every Gain
Every Venture, Every Pain

Every Step, Every Way
Every End, Every Day

Every Page, Every Chapter
Every Book, Every Disaster

Every Travesty, Every Fight
Every Belief, Every Plight

Every Memory, Every Reflection
Every Time was paved with good intention

She is Laura

Small by design but big on personality
She is a gust of wind that swirls around us but is a breeze by our side
Laughter emanates from her heart as humility allows her to share
Comfortable in herself she owes nothing to anyone

Free from scripture she is independent in thought
A gentle smile and teasing eyes she leaves you wondering
Easy-going her sense of humour invites you to be yourself
Honest in conversation she whispers gently her ideals

She does resist when necessary but is open to temptation
Humble in company she lifts the spirits of those around her
A willingness to embrace the new she exhibits no fear
Alive with generosity her calming influence beguiles you

Her passion obvious it is tempered with empathy for those less fortunate
A delicate but firm presence gives way to an unmistakable vulnerability
Her delight at things so simple gives rise to an open heart
Her mannerism encourages others to seek solace in her

Ambition she covets in carefully crafted but sensitive plans
A free spirit she shapes her own path yet is open to persuasion
She brings tenderness and sensuality to any situation
She beckons you to her side in the only way a French accent can

Her words alluring, her mind mischievous, she causes ripples in our heart
We're alive to her nature, one of kindness, one of openness, one that serenades you
She is gentle, she is warm, she is humble, she is sexy, she is here, she is Laura

You know who you are

Yip, the person who parks across two parking spaces coz your car is more important than ours, you know who you are

Yip, the person who parks in a disabled bay because you're lazy and couldn't be arsed to walk the length of yourself, you know who you are

Yip, the person who will actually throw rubbish out of your car onto the street because it will remove the bad look from your car, you know who you are

Yip, the person who will tear up trees for no other reason than you can, you know who you are

Yip, the person who will randomly abuse someone in the street because you assume your friends are an audience, you know who you are

Yip, the person who answers the phone in a meeting because your interests take precedence over everyone else, you know who you are

Yip, the person who drives into a parking space when you've been patiently waiting on it because their needs are greater, you know who you are

Yip, the person who is happy to let others buy drinks but fails to put his hand in his pocket because taking advantage doesn't cost you a thought, you know who you are

Yip, the person who puts all their bags on the seat beside them because you don't want to entertain the idea of a stranger sitting beside you, you know who you are

Yip, the person who likes to start arguments or dishes out treatment to others but is aghast when we express our opinion, you know who you are

Yip, the person who finds excuse to berate others to simply draw attention away from your own failings, you know who you are

Yip, the person who plants the seeds of discontent among others yet hides among the crowd, you know who you are

Yip, the person who speaks loudest yet whose motivation is not about reason but agenda, you know who you are

Yip, the person who subtly leans against you at the bar so you'll make space for them, you know who you are

Yip, the person whose child is guilty of nothing because you give him everything to make up for something, you know who you are

Yip, the person who always finds excuse to rationalise every barrier to disguise your issues and shortcomings, you know who you are

Yip, the person who has a view on every subject and dismisses any critique as conjecture, you know who you are

Yip, the person who is prepared to argue the case but does a Pontius Pilate when it goes wrong, yes my friends you all know who you are, we all know who you are

Intimacy can be

Intimacy can be a whisper in the ear
It can be a glance at your rear
It can be a gentle brush of your hand
It can be an intense kiss on the strand

It can be pillow talk at night
It can be the passion after a fight
It can be a horny conversation
It can be limitless exploration

It can be a stroke of your hair
It can be sitting together on one chair
It can be a film and a glass of red
It can be a cuddle in bed

It can be an arm around your waist
It can be caressing you without haste
It can be sharing a candle lit evening
It can be a shared movie screening

It can be lying together in a bath
It can be a spontaneous laugh
It can be not knowing your mind
It can be searching to see what I can find

It can be all of these and more
It can be what we are longing for
It can be just what we want it to be
But most of all it can be just you and me

Another book of poems by Fergal Barr 21

The Majestic Miss Looney

It was less than 48 hours but none I will forget
A lifetime of honesty crammed into two days such was the effect
A moving array of emotion that cannot be defined
A senseless wander into surreal that simply blew our minds

Arriving with such expectation was always laced with risk
Carrying the burden of differing emotions sealed in that first kiss
The desires that revealed themselves prior to our meet
Seem to unravel in an instant as they lay at our feet

Not realising I had lost you before we'd even begun
I had to send out a rescue mission to prevent you going home
My thoughts articulated 'wisely' in that 'special' kind of advice
Feeling I owe you my honesty was like being cut with a knife

'I cannot believe my ears; doesn't she see what she means?'
This sudden new reality like something from a bad dream
How the hell did this happen and when did it come to pass?
What can I do to convince her that flight is not a path?

The feelings that got us here are worth more than we probably know
And even if there's a new realisation we don't have to let it go
Because when you find someone who makes you tick you really feel alive
It's not surprising then when you want to be at their side

Of course i'm not foolish and the risks I always knew
But a logical mind doesn't always compute that one plus one doesn't always make two
And so here I am wondering now what will happen next
And what I learned from a situation seemingly so complex

This is not a story about something I have lost
But rather a reflection on a story of someone I found I can trust
You see I met this beautiful lady just a few years ago
And never thought for one second I stand with her toe to toe

She is not merely just beauty but that of course is true
She laughs and giggles like a teenager hell bent on sharing it with you
She is gentle in demeanour but firm in her praise
She will walk with you in difficulties and seduce you with her gaze

She is sensitive in your company but honest when it's time
She does not pander to some awful pretence but shares with you her mind
She is daring and adventurous and harbours a creative twist
She requires a strong independent someone to remain on her 'potentials' list

She is homely where it matters and knows what is just and fair
She doesn't suffer fools gladly, nothing to repair
She knows what she wants and no appeal does she entertain
She likes the cheeky, the challenging and the forward but nothing so vein

So in the time that I've known her what can I honestly say?
Little or nothing negative, not even a sarcastic foray
For she is that potent combination of beauty, intelligence and personality
And with every moment spent with her a step further from neutrality

You see she doesn't just grab your attention, she positively holds your court
She steals your momentary weakness as she beguiles you with witty retort
She playfully embraces your vulnerability never threatening your sense of self
Rather standing with you in unison offering you a supportive hand to help

You see you can't remain unaffected nor detached when spending time with she
Aloofness, impartiality and neutrality are not on the agenda when with thee
Your warmth, your friendship, your passion and your care are as natural as they come
Your laughter, your perspective, your honesty and tenderness rise and fall with the sun

And as I write this and contemplate forever the possibility
I am tempered with thoughts of what became reality
Because a woman like you are seldom in our midst and this I mean, Truly
What a wonderful time with the beautiful and The Majestic Miss Looney

Out of the blue

Out of the blue she emerged
A moment not sponsored by regret
Forthright in conviction, steadfast in belief
She gambles, she pays, she is rewarded

She wonders how this moment will be received
Quietly confident, curiously nervous, excitement in waiting
He doesn't get it at first, 'no it couldn't be, sure she is already content and happy'
Questions and answers, explanations and clarifications, hopes and declarations

The mist clears as rays of sunshine shed new light
Past connections given new insight and life
Ignorance is bliss they say and it is now that there's a new show in town
A show that has just lifted its curtain and where the protagonists wait in the wings

The music begins, the stage is prepared, characters wait for their cue, the lights go on
From the shadows players converge as the scene is set
An exchange of lines, pronounced intentions, the plot thickens
Consumed by passion and desire, emotions are laid bare as discretion gives way to honesty

This is no longer a story of a once nearly something
Much more is at stake here, no neat lines of symmetry and affability
Any pretence governed by the past cast aside as senses are aroused
Tension builds as mere attraction is overtaken by depth and meaning

No longer merely a scene or a play the script is unedited
The actors granted artistic licence as they command the stage
'Improv' doesn't do it justice as they don't choose their lines carefully but rather playfully
They're in the moment, lost in the candour of their feelings

She made a play, he wants a part
She has caused a scene, he never saw it coming
She handed him a script, he's rehearsing it like crazy
She picks the cast, he wants the lead part

She is front and centre, he waits in the wings
She captivates an audience, he has front row tickets
She bows before no-one, he catches her eye
She appeals with gesture, he responds in kind

The audience is forgotten as they lure one another with fantasy
Their minds in parity as they wrestle with desire
They want each other and no journey is too far, no requests too great
New possibilities as the last lines are recited

The curtain drops to the floor as do the clothes that once adorned them
They don't see limitations as they explore one another with zeal and vigour
Passionate beads of sweat inch slowly
But wait, a different story line, a smaller cast, a change of scenery, a new oration

In which direction are they headed as they reach out to instinct?
What guarantees are there as no man's land beckons?
How possible to sustain such craving as demons gather?
The past not standing on ceremony as it trundles headlong towards them

What hope a new love as one sees only the present?
What possibility a new era as one sees only the future?
What compromises await as common ground is sought?
What flowers can blossom in a moment beset by drought?

What spring yields eternal where both do not see through one lens?
What purpose is served where gratification cannot embrace a new love?
What intention gives way to a future with a recollection of passion but no compassion?
What future lies in a sticky resolve of release and appeasement to placate a desire for pay back?

What emotional security is to be gleaned from a black and white existence?
What principles are to be sacrificed in a bid to avenge a grievance?
What possible heartache lies in wait when your wishes are met?
What do you lose when you become a parody of yourself?

What reflection stares at you in your mirror of needs only?
What do you seek to rid yourself off to make peace with what's gone before?
What will you forego to pursue a greener, grassier mould on the other side?
What for them now as the crossroads emerge in the distance?

How can he translate his love for her into a permanent stay of execution?
How can she look beyond the gallows of options to preserve a life that resonates?
Is there to be another time, another place, another try?
In her hand she holds love in his time

What a world we live in

Immigrants drowning at sea on a boat of desperation
Neighbours who cut each other down with the knives of political difference
Young people who take their own lives as resilience gives way to cyber trolls

Men who use females as toys of rape in a meaningless gung-ho battle over territory
Predators that covet children for their own gratuitous sexual pleasures
The greedy that become weighed down by the burden of financing their ego

Church aficionados who extol virtues to live by to deter gazing eyes from their own fallables
Politicians who lead us to believe yet corrupt us with their divisive mantras
Poverty that culls human after human in a resource laden world

Government that talks only about small changes in inflation yet is a brutal tax over time
Truth seekers who are hounded and persecuted in order to protect the interests of the few
Fuel fanatics who will crack open the earth at the risk of making a permanent irreversible mark

Teachers who cradle learning yet lose sight of the reason why they are there in the first place
Property dealers and estate agents who see only pounds signs as the homeless see only eviction notices
Business fraternity who see only children as a bulge in their wallet

Traffickers who trade in contempt for humanity
Lawyers who uphold and defend the law of 'it's the law'
Media who see only sexy in the negative

Dissidents who perceive only a garden of Eden whilst the rest of us see only a barren wasteland
Protestors who assert their brother rights but forget their first cousin responsibility
Parents who cherish their children but fail to lead as they refuse to emerge from the shadow of their teenage indulgence

Reality TV producers who have succeeded in removing us further and further from reality
The Adult World who offer us numerous examples yet demonise children when they follow suit
Pessimists who like to make points and buy space and time but refuse to trade in the currency of optimism

The serious who want us to share their cause but are unable to share even a smile
The righteous that choose to judge but hide from view when history wants to paint their portrait
The 10% who own 90% yet fear the 90% who have to share the 10%
What a world we live in

I don't get it, I just don't get it

She approached me, not me approaching her
I didn't make any obvious signs or noises
I was just doing my own thing
Minding my own business, taking care of my own stuff

I knew who she was but she didn't know me, how could she, no reason for her to know
But she still approached me inquiring 'have we met before?'
'No' I said, I knew we hadn't but I said 'I know who you are'

She asked was I involved in her line of business
'No' I said, 'but I'm deeply passionate about it'
'Maybe we could meet up some day for a chat....I have some ideas'
'Have you got an e-mail?'

I handed her pen & paper, she gave me her e-mail and number
Why I thought? I wasn't complaining, but why? Why her number? I am still a stranger to her
I made a point of not asking
I'd only be disappointed, I mean she didn't know me, she'd only just met me, why?

Perhaps it was more, perhaps she liked me, and after all she approached me out of the blue
No initiation, no conversation, no logical reason to do so, just cause I sat across from her, but hey
I sit across from people every day and it doesn't happen
But she just did, 'people tend to be more shy here than in London' I recall she said
Interesting, maybe it's true, maybe we're more wary here

And thus we met again for coffee, for tea, for conversation, for sharing, for sharing our stories
A sincere honesty prevailed, a real in-depth sharing – some of her story I was blown away by
I couldn't match it, I didn't really try, just offered glimpses of my past, my life, my context, my own struggles

I thought wow this is great, meeting someone and having such an in-depth conversation about 'stuff,'
never had such a quality of conversation in such a long time
Boy I miss that, I miss that kind of conversation, that sense of compassion
It's fulfilling, it gives you something, it rallies the soul, it fills a number of gaps, it simply makes sense
It offers hope, it suggests belief, it nurtures energy, it helps you imagine

I have my work but I work on my own
I have my kids but I'm really a sounding board for their future endeavours, a catch-up for them,
a place they can vent their spleen and a safety net in times of need
I have my football which provides the banter I need, an outlet for frustrations and energy, a means of escapism
I have my friends for the banal, the conjecture, the frustrations, the assertions and the like

But no-one specifically where the weight and density of conversation is akin to the inner and outer layers of this planet
I thought wouldn't this be nice to continue this conversation over a drink some time
I suggested we did - we never met again for a coffee or tea after that!
That I just don't get

Another book of poems by Fergal Barr

Madiba

I raise a glass to you, there's no need to shed a tear
We knew this moment would come but ease the loss it does not
Words do not come close, actions seem futile, thoughts are lost, tributes are among many, how can I truly let you know what you meant?

I can't now, I can only dream of you at the dinner table, just to be in your company, just to sit in your presence, just to touch you, to know heroes are not only real but humble

In a decade of anniversaries, memories mark the past, commemorations approach and have passed, you're well beyond your 50th, chalked up your 90th, never made your 100th

Even the quarter of a century since your release is still some time away, your passing doesn't coincide with anniversaries or commemorations but that is your measure – you stand out yet you embed the essence of all, each day filled with love, humility, compassion and peace

I used to toil, protest, react, argue – I tried to convince, persuade, coerce those not convinced by the actions of the regime you rallied against, I did it from afar as best I could but I upheld your call, I stood against the pirates of dishonesty, I was young, this is what I knew, I held you in esteem, I called your name, I wanted the world, my world to know what a horrible heinous regime it was

I wanted to turn people away from the products of suppression, from those who could care but continue to peddle, Nelson I fought as only a young teenager who when in a position to do so, in the outside world, I fought as I could, I fought in a patch that I might be able to sway people in

And when you were released I sat still, I watched you emerge in your beautiful suit, glanced at the black and white picture, the last but most famous one we had, the only one we all had, I couldn't quite see you in him as you walked gracefully across our TV screens, when there was only 4 channels but all seem to capture that moment, all seemed glued to it, but of course it was you, it was you, there was no doubt, it was you

I listened, I celebrated, I rejoiced, I exalted in what you had to say, hung on your every word, not a message of pain, revenge, or even joy of release, but one of peace, love, reconciliation, one of compassion, turning the other cheek, embracing your neighbour

Mandela, Mandela, Mandela....Madiba, Madiba, Madiba, very few of this generation will really understand, will really comprehend

I never met you but I tried to walk in your footseps, I never talked to you but I tried to share your message, I never lived with you but I tried to live in your way, I will never see you again but I won't let your message go

Love is a very confusing thing

Love is a very confusing thing
It can pick you up and take you places yet drop you anywhere
It can elevate you to a higher plain yet leave you feeling low
It can take your breath away yet leave you gasping for air

Love is a very confusing thing
It encourages you to believe yet leaves your beliefs in pieces
It can indulge you in an instant yet expel you in a flash
It can take you to fields of gold yet yield no harvest

Love is a very confusing thing
It requires you to be honest yet induces fear of the truth
It necessitates your complete understanding yet leaves you feeling misunderstood
It demands that you make many sacrifices yet can hang you out to dry

Love is a very confusing thing
It can add a spring to your step yet trip you along the way
It can open up so many doors yet be the ground that swallows you up
It can be the treasure you've always sought yet fritter your investment away

Love is a very confusing thing
It asks you to be patient yet expects you to endure without question
It delivers many packages to your doorstep without instructions for assembly
It throws you many lifelines but leaves you still wishing you had phoned a friend

Love is a very confusing thing
It can be the inspiration you've longed for yet devour your aspirations
It contrives to throw many different options at you but only succeeds in offering the wrong one
It asks you to commit for eternity yet we know no-one has ever lived that long

Love is a very confusing thing
It encourages you to make promises to yourself yet watches you disintegrate when you break one
It instils in you a conviction for love yet leaves you feeling convicted when charged
It motivates you to believe that there is someone out there yet they never reveal themselves

Love is indeed a very confusing thing

When they've gone

There is no-one really left to talk to any more, when all is said and done they've all gone
The music still plays but the glasses lie empty, there are no shadows on the wall any more, no fireside tales, no heartfelt pleas, no momentary gestures, no chitter-chatter

Only tunes of delight act as a savoury companion against the gathering night skies
A means of bridging the present and the past where bodies occupied the now suspended moment

Piped music surrounds the dimly lit lobby, a comfortable noise that offers sustenance to the nothingness, the nothingness that gave way to the personless, the personless that left only a disturbing calm, the disturbing calm that is first cousin of the yet to be visited loneliness

The quiet room, the empty space, the echo of assertions, the faint sound of footsteps, the laughter tones, the click, the clink and the chime of glasses all just a fading noise

The emptiness of the moment exacerbated by what was, what has passed, what still lingers, the plans, the promises, the actions, the commitments, the beliefs, the desires to meet again

A space created, gaps filled, lines crossed, ambitions realised, questions posed, ideas generated, all a testament to a moment in time when people where first and foremost

A handful of cars lie stationery, a statement of intent, waiting to be ignited and seeking purpose
They belong to no-one yet someone, they belong to memories, when they've gone they're gone

Some accidents

Some accidents leave no injury, are not fatal, do not break us, have not scarred us, pain us not nor take our breath...

Some accidents steal our affection, quicken our reaction, wake us from our slumber, spark us into life, protect us from ourselves and soften our impact....

Some accidents were meant to be, are determined by fate, are already in place, are influenced by no-one, have no ulterior motive, are not a conspiracy nor are they designed against us....

Some accidents shine a light upon us, give us the attention we crave, grant us the wishes we desire, give us the excuse we were looking for, allow us to wallow but do not forgive us in people's minds....

Some accidents invite us to change, dictate our next steps, make us take control, force a new reality, engage us in persuasion, enlist our commitment, ignite our passion yet question our convictions....

Some accidents drive you, give you reason to live, to run faster, to make a difference, to show who's the boss, to nurture an energy, to curate a dream, to create a space but not hold people to ransom...

Some accidents bring us to the edge, lay siege to our beliefs, question our values, scoff at our principles, pour scorn on ideals, crucify our intention, deride our endeavours but fail to bring us to heel....

Some accidents will happen to you, will pass you by, will ride alongside you, will catapult you into the centre, will fall short of you at the last moment but all of them will make you the person you are.

The Sores on our landscape

The sores on our landscape, oh what a pitiful harvest we sew, where buildings steeped in the grounds of heavy investment clamour to compete in a sky line of sliver, glass and metal yet the doors remain permanently closed to those who have to scavenge in their shadow, the sleek lines of industrial endeavour a testimony to the rich indulgence of the few whilst the many can only dream of making decisions without having to think about them ever again

The sores on our landscape remain steadfast as the penniless, the homeless, the poverty-stricken, the deranged, the hopeless, the beggars, the needy and the desperate mix their trades among the elite hoping for that golden moment, that big break, that second chance to lift them from the gloom, to exhume them from the dead streets, to catapult them into a new reality, to speed them on their way, to allow them to walk noticed among others

The sores on the landscape haven't gone away you know, haven't de-materialised, haven't disappeared, haven't become invisible, they've laid waste to the hopes and ambitions of generations who are left to harbour only simple pleasures whilst losing their sanity, screaming on the inside but silent on the outside, pleading for just one of our busy moments, as our body language strains to avoid and our eyes quickly avert their sunken gaze

The sores on our landscape continue unhindered as the tills still ring, the restaurants still cook, the banks still cash, the financiers still chuckle, the politicians still cosy up to one another, as the planners still decide, as the industrials still plot, as the managers still hire, as the workers still endeavour, as the lights still flicker, as the meek still cup grains of sand

The sores on our landscape testify against nobody, account for nothing, apologise to no-one, justify to anyone who will listen, can explain it all away, will not seek redemption, won't let it happen again, can advise others on how to avoid it yet will not be imprisoned by their actions nor fall by their sword of indulgence nor live the lives of those whose pleas they ignored

The sores on our landscape make promises, offer their condolences, extend their best wishes, cry their crocodile tears but somehow are still with us, they somehow still survive, somehow have come through, are born again, are once more indulged, whilst the plague that engulfed them, surrounded them, threatened them was chastised by an injection of public wealth stolen from our future nest eggs, plundered from our past endeavours, scrambled from our beliefs in the institutions that are, will be and regrettably are still the sores on our landscape

The Internal Angst

The Internal Angst in my head grates me no more
The conflicting opinions that aroused my temper breathe silently
The battles that raged inside me have swallowed their pride
The demons that interned me have relinquished their crown

The debt I carried has lost its value
The burden of necessity was merely an illusion of my own making
The seat of deception has been crushed under the weight of its own righteousness
The feelings of isolation is drowned out by the noise of someone caring

The explanation of others was only brought to me by the empty promises of history
The ground that was always going uphill has been levelled by a stronger emotion
The fickle nature of the selfish has been cast aside in favour of the selfless
The carefully crafted opinions have been banished to the sidelines of the meaningless

The illusions of grandeur exhibited by others is replaced by the seduction of humility
The currency of the highfliers cannot be exchanged for the wealth of generosity
The lies of the fearful are not worthy of retort
The determination of those anxious to be first does not merit competition

The assertions of the judgemental reflects only their inability to be at peace
The 'I showed them' approach of the assertive is merely confused with aggression
The flattery of the insincere is a tool that yields limited progress
The deliberations of the social media generation is oblivious to the inertia of their musings

The exaggeration of the needy is to be viewed as an invite for some TLC
The speculation of the power hungry is to be left wilting in the heat of the moment
The irony of the law makers is to be upheld in the courts of public gaze
The nausea of the power brokers is only to be tempered by ridicule

I guess not...

Like the coffee stained cups
The switch to knock the heating on
The sound of the stereo in the background
The presence of the footsteps upstairs
The car pulling up outside – could it be they have returned?

A scent that lingers in the bedroom
The Guinness stained Kronenberg glass
The tools and the left over tiles
The birthday decoration
The flow of tea and coffee

Left over chinese and lemons
The natural yoghurts
The photographs
The nice touches you brought
The music we shared

Relaxing feet up on the sofa
The left behind Max strength
The sound of loneliness takes hold
The complete and absolute feeling of emptiness
The house without presence

Waiting for you to walk through the kitchen door
The internal struggles of feelings and thoughts
The complete lack of company
The remaining beer cans
The regret and anger of falling asleep

An inability to deal with emotion
The anguish and pain in my heart
The loneliness of not knowing
The knowing it's probably a dream

Who is she?

Young she may be but grace is second nature
Consideration is often in short supply but humility she has in abundance
Coarse words is the script of many but gentle tender is her language
Sadness besets person after person but laughter is her currency

Despair consumes those less able but hope she nurtures eternally
Impatience is the tenure of the intolerant but time she devotes without question
Heartache is a burden that we all endure but learning to accept its pain she embraces
Circumstance is a paralysis for some but she draws strength from it

Beauty overcomes many but she is comfortable with such platitudes bestowed upon her
Vice is a temptation that greets us all but thoughtful disposition is her natural habitat
Loss of control is a deluge we will encounter but a sense of temperance she musters
Lack of gratitude is a modern accompaniment but heartfelt thanks is her last post and chorus

Compassion is beyond those who preach loudest but embedded in her demeanour
Sensitivity is out of reach for many yet she touches those she meets
Dignity is merely a thought to some but she walks in its footsteps every day
Caring is a mountain to climb for the indulgent but a walk in the park for her

Adversity is a millstone to many a weary neck but she does not choke at its prospect
Generosity escapes lesser souls but her spirit ensures no such fate
Sincerity is a mask wore by the impatient but a state of mind to she
Love is a condition for the inept but a comfort she shares even with strangers

Compromise is a loss of face to the judgemental but a matter of conviction for her
Fairness is not on the radar of the angry but a sense of belonging for her
Passion is an extreme for the impetuous but a reason for her to exist
Belief is a value to be sold by the greedy but to her it's a commodity not for tendering

A smile, a laugh and a desire to be more than is a stretch too far for some but for Katie Brown it's the only way....that's who she is....

Garrett so Smarrett

Garrett so Smarrett, a young man of reputable heart
For he bleeds not lightly but takes all in his stride
Defender in the Norse Universe and Strong Spear in the English World
He calmly leads and suffers fools not gladly

Commitment he bringeth to the kingdom of red cards
By mean tenure he tolerate no demeaning of humanity
But scolds those who leave integrity at their feet

He is of gentle persuasion but firm compassion
Yet forgiving and caring of those who wish to share his cause

His desire is noble & defends the honour of those who suffer at the words of the ignorant
A pavilion of light in a dark episode of racism he yields not to the intolerance of the few but shows fair hand in the love of humanity

But a meek and simple being he tends not a lonely furrow but rejoices in the righteousness of his sense of right from wrong – tidings will carry you far.

Have I ever......?

Have I ever assaulted anyone?
Only if a fight in the playground constitutes assault

Have I ever stolen from someone?
If you define stealing as taking something without permission then yes but hasn't everyone and it was a long time ago and I learned it was wrong

Have I ever lied?
Yes....but a long time ago and I grew to realise it was futile not to mention wrong

Have I ever cheated?
Yes...but a long time ago and I am older and wiser now and know there is no virtue in it and I just get more pleasure from being honest

Have I ever set out to hurt anyone?
Maybe at school but that was when I was a kid and didn't know any better

Have I ever killed anyone?
No and don't intend to

Have I ever raped anyone?
No and such an act wouldn't ever cross my mind

Do I go out of my way to insult or offend?
No but sometimes I do without realising it but apologise when I do

Do I pick fights?
No, I don't like violence and let's face it what's the point really?

Am I greedy?
No, I don't like it but of course I would like a little more in my life

Am I dishonest?
No....I endeavour to be as honest as I can

Do I get it wrong sometime?
Well of course....who doesn't but I try to put it right when I do

Am I 'man' enough to apologise when I get wrong?
I do, I've done and will continue to do so even when I feel inclined not to

So tell me why are there still some who are more than a little obsessed with pointing the finger at me and making judgements?
Why are there always these people out there?
Why is it we take notice of them only to discover they were least best-placed to judge anyone?
Why do we never learn to ignore them?
It's time to start....

If I was in love with you

If I was in love with you I'd care for you so much they'd have to dig deep to reach me
I'd care for you so much I'd feel the pain even when only you hurt
I'd care for you unlike any other even though we're surrounded by people we love
I'd care for you with a desire that no invention could possibly measure

I'd care for you so strongly I'd want to reach out and touch you even when I'm miles from nowhere
I'd care for you so entirely that I would not see others even if they are stood right in front of me
I'd care for you so emphatically that everything is on the table
I'd care for you in a way that leaves you not even having to ask

I'd care for you so much that a day would never pass where I wouldn't ask you so
I'd care for you so tightly they would have to untangle me
I'd care for you so much that I would write it into history
I'd care for you so much that you wouldn't need to ask again

I'd care for you so much that you would hear it in my breathing
I'd care for you so carefully that every move is carefully choreographed
I'd care for you so much that if it was written on a wall it would stand out among the graffiti
I'd care for you so much that every gamble taken is not a risk but a leap of faith

I'd care for you so much that every question is a reason to share
I'd care for you so much that every uncertainty is only a story to convince you so
I'd care for you so much that every absence is an invite to be in your presence
I'd care for you so much that every day is a gift beyond value

I'd care for you so much that when the doubts come I would seek your counsel
I'd care for you so much that when you lose patience I will find another way
I'd care for you so much that when you struggle for air I will breathe for you
I'd care for you so much that when they hand out crowns I will relinquish mine

The Government

The Government led people, encouraged people, supported people, threw money at people and at the first sign of trouble evicted people from their homes

The Government encourage, support, entice, persuade and convince people that the best way to pay is by DD's yet hammer people when they miss one

The Government encourage you to take out insurance for this, for that and when you go to claim you discover you don't fulfil the right conditions

The Government asked you, supported you, encouraged you to plan for the future, take out a pension, enjoy your retirement, to which you bought into only for it to be declared worthless

The Government encouraged you, supported you, advised you to take your money out of the mattress and give it to the banks only to discover your mattress doesn't try to cheat you

The Government led you to believe, asked you to trust, convinced you to buy into, cajoled you into supporting a justice system that only the wealthy can buy themselves out off

The Government enticed you, invited you, persuaded you, left you with no option but to seek work that makes pay spineless

The Government led you to believe, convinced you to support, argued strongly with you to endorse, promised you it was worth the effort to fight for equality yet still finds reason to deny rights for many

The Government advocates on your behalf, encourages us to live by strong charitable values, hounds you to reconcile with others, guilts you into loving your neighbour yet does not stand up to those who oppose love between some neighbours

The Government went to you, invited you to come here, promised you a place to stay, encouraged you to settle yet now it wants to send you home

The Government sold you a dream, encouraged everyone to buy, motivated you to set up, enticed you with the money that didn't belong to them and are now happy for you to stagnate in negative equity

The Government encouraged you to be more flexible, asked you to sacrifice more, assured you we're all in this together, promised you things would get better yet did nothing to stop costs spiralling

The Government......Bastards!

Doesn't he remember?

Doesn't he remember the smile that was alluring?
Doesn't he remember the smile that greeted him in the morning?
Doesn't he remember the long flowing hair that washed over her shoulders, a beautiful dark mane silhouetting against the early morning sunshine?
Doesn't he remember the smile that greeted him in the morning, doesn't he remember her sensitivity, her open book, her dreams she shared, her soul she bared?

Doesn't he remember the gentle, humble easy-going nature that became rampant and passionate as they shared the night?
Doesn't he remember the conversations, the connections, the promises, the look deep into her eyes that said no matter what, it's here, it's now, it won't change, it will come again?
Doesn't he remember why he came there in the first place?
Doesn't he remember why he chose her? Doesn't he remember anything?

Doesn't he want to share it again?
Doesn't he want to know what it would be like once more?
Doesn't he see what he's missing?
Doesn't he want to be part of something that was beautiful, something that stood for something, something that meant more than the night, something that moved, something that breathed life, something that was in the moment?

Clearly not.....but he will remember one day it was his loss!

As if Lior was my light

A smile that can positively melt
A curiosity that is often heart felt
A charm that beguiles many a soul
A warmth that carries no toll

Compassion that knows no bounds
A companion that listens for every sound
A mind that wants to know more
A love that doesn't keep score

A loyalty that remains clear
A belief that shows no fear
A sensitivity that leaves you in no doubt
A sensuality that wears you out

Tenderness that greets you every day
A beauty that surrounds you in every way
An instinct just and fair
She is indeed a breath of fresh air

How Can I.....

How can I convince you of what I feel?
How can I help you believe it is genuine and real?
How can I convey to you what is in my heart?
How can I ask you to consider a fresh start?

How can I try to make it up to you somehow over time?
How can I reverse the mess I created in your mind?
How can I reassure you that you are nothing like a clown?
How can I express what you mean to me whenever you're around?

How can I convince you to let go just one more time?
How can I reassure you I will be clearer in my mind?
How can I offer you something worthwhile to believe in?
How can I bring back to you that loving feeling?

How can I get us back to where it was?
How can I reassure you about my human flaws?
How can I get you to make one last stand?
How can I persuade you to once again take my hand?

How can I show you that it's worth one more try?
How can I convince you of what I see when I look at you with my eyes?
How can I find the words that will bring you back?
How can I create the feeling that we're somehow back on track?

How can I persuade you of all that was good?
How can I convince you that all I said and felt were true?
How can I help to ease your anger and pain?
How can I win your desire to be with me once again?

How can I remind you of what we had just a short time ago?
How can I remind you it happened because we both let go?
How can I convince you that feeling is worth fighting for?
How can I convince you not to close this particular door?

How can I persuade you to let me find another way?
How can I convince you to let me hold you another day?
How can I persuade you to share another bottle of wine?
And how can I convince you to try one more time?

The fisherman and the mermaid

The fisherman told me he met this beautiful mermaid
And when he saw her he turned off his engine
Dropped anchor and reeled in his nets
He put a chair at the front of his boat and against the sun
He watched his mermaid play in the water creating many beautiful moments

The fisherman told me that when he looks at this mermaid he sees how beautiful she is
That he often skips a little breath thinking about it
He loves her smile
He loves her gentle nature
Her honesty
Her humility
He loves that she keeps him grounded
He loves to be with her
He loves the idea of being with her
He knows she's not always at his side but senses her presence because he has watched her closely many times
Even when she doesn't notice

And when absent he remembers the moments and relives them in his mind and heart
He loves the idea of sailing unchartered waters with her
He loves her sense of humour and that she laughs with him
He loves hanging out with the mermaids own little mermaids
He loves that she isn't pretentious and she doesn't pretend to be anything other than a mermaid
He loves the fact that she accepts the fisherman for who he is
The fact she is also his friend and looks out for him
He loves her beauty and how he makes him feel

It was then that he knew that even though the ocean was full of fish
He couldn't see them any more beyond the vision that was before him
He upped anchor, raised his sail and let the wind carry him with his mermaid to unchartered waters....

Pleasing Others - Part I

We spend our entire childhood being told what we should do or be
We spend out entire adolescence being convinced about what we can have and have not
We spend out entire adulthood being persuaded about we should take or leave
And now, we will spend out entire later life being chased for what we have and what we don't have

But I have toiled and endeavoured
I have given my lot and asked for only mere recognition in return
I have paid my dues, my taxes and filed my returns yet robbed of my dignity when I needed you most
I have scrimped and saved and relied upon my meagre resources yet every year I'm told to find more

I have walked, I have run, I have danced and sprinted yet the finishing line is a mirage in the desert
I have stood in line, waited my turn, bided my time yet the shudders come down when I reach the top
I have kept my word, fulfilled my promises, followed the crowd yet the clouds have no bronze never mind silver lining
I have rallied, spoken out in defence of, forsaken my own yet made a pariah when the spotlight was on you

I have lived by the rules, bought into your ideals, upheld your beliefs yet discover you share none of my values
I have walked the walk, talked the talk yet you do not walk alongside me nor hear my voice when I scream
I have lived the good life, dismissed temptation and given myself to others yet I still await my 15 minutes
I have asked for little, demanded nothing and sought solace yet you still expect more and more and more each day

A Portrait of Tina

Every now and then someone enters your life
And takes a moment of your time yet stays for quite a while
Robbing you of your attention as if you had nothing else to do
Patiently waiting with more than just a warm embrace

Lingering in your thoughts a little longer as if out of nowhere
Quietly relieving you of your stress as their kindness undermines you
As if they had no right to but you're grateful anyway
Life standing still but you're not the same without it

A warm smile, a gentle touch, a knowing look
A thoughtful gaze, a sensitive word, a daring mind
A hearty laugh, a desirable intent, an intimate feeling
An encouragable past, a passionate encounter, a future undecided

Unmatched in care and unconditional in love you gave no second thought
Cradling in compassion and undaunted by your past
You give fully of yourself without pretence or obstacle
Sacrificing self-interest as only selflessness can

Holding firm to the values you espouse you will not forsake
Truly principled to the end you know your destiny
Life might dictate but agitate for change you will
Certain of what you want and careful of what you need

Handling many destinies is a matter of every day course
Caring for others is as natural as your smile
Fun-filled summer-like days you crave
Friendship is an open book with many sunny chapters yet unwritten

Not wanting to forget yet longing to move on
Your passion burns brightly in the midst of your dreams
Striking out to reach where the heart yearns
The words of your soul written in your pointed looks

You entered my life without warning creating special moments
Lingering memories hung on playful intent harbour heartfelt emotions
Being part of this journey we were passengers craving for an unhindered view
We gathered together often without care or concern

Blue skies dominated and wrote memories in the whites of the cloud
Rain, snow or shine could not unsettle a gentle breeze
Yet stronger winds carried us in different directions
But friendship is the shadow that we eternally walk in

When I think about.....I remember

When I have been unemployed I remember I have worked most of my adult life
When I have been a little under the weather I remember I have never been seriously ill
When I have aches, pains and strains I remember I can walk, I can run, I can hide
When I have felt alone I remember I still have family

When I have struggled financially I remember I have never truly lived in poverty
When I have longed for more I remember the wait is making me a better person
When I have been rejected I remember that I'm not the only one
When I have lost I remember how it ensures I take nothing for granted

When I have been wrong I remember it taught me humility
When I have been certain I remember to assume nothing
When I have been excluded I remember there must be a reason
When I have been forgotten I remember there are others who don't

When I have been dishonest I remember I'm not being true to myself
When I have snapped I remember that's the memory people will be left with
When I have gloated I remember it is always short-lived
When I have boasted I remember others will seek to out-boast me

When I have been angry I remember I have already lost
When I have been down I remember the only way is up
When I have been dismissive I remember how it felt
When I have been envious I remember that everyone should have their moment

When I have been jealous I remember my time will come
When I have been at my lowest I remember there are others worse off than me
When I have been tempted I remember others will remind me
When I take shortcuts I remember someone had to travel the long way around first

When I have nothing I remember I have more than most
When I have no more laughter I remember that a day without laughter is a day lost
When I have to stand up and be counted I remember those that came before me
When I forget what I have learned I remember that each day is a school day

Waiting

I'm only good enough to sit among my own company
That's it, just me, nothing else
Time to go home, nothing worth waiting for
Loneliness prevails, wish I could show everyone else, something else, something new,
neither borrowed nor blue

Time is slow, it paces up and down
It moves from this room to that room
It has no plans, no agenda, no decisions to make, no journeys to take
Yet it is all of this and more

Tomorrow will be different
A new day, a new start, a new resilience
Adulation and excitement in small things to merely generate momentum
To gather pace, to feel desire and ignite passions, to kill time, fill a vacuum,
offset that which might consume

Sun greets the morning, peeks through the blinds
The sound of stillness is real, alive, unbroken
Promises form overhead, this will be the day
A day of non-reckoning, a day much like yesterday

Sixteen hours to go
How will I manage?
What can I dream up, what can I add to my list?
What unexpected moments can I expect?

Pages to turn, reading to get lost
More musings to collate
New knowledge to gather, to get by, to get ready
Gotta go deeper, can't break the monotony

Pen to paper, gentle ink blotting a new page
Blue in colour, cool in stature, resolute in defiance
Sourcing meaning as ink blazes a trail
Defining a new story, a new narrative, a new inspiration

The day passes, hours ticked off, promises unveiled, knowledge gained
Ideas closer to reality, dreams kept alive, lists added to
The unexpected never failing to surprise, survival achieved, feet up
Soul enriched, tomorrow we start again, time passes
I'm still waiting

I wanna live in a country

I wanna live in a country where the flag I stand under is embraced by all
I wanna live in a country where the policies that govern us are dictated not by religious doctrine or political ideology but determined by logic and reason
I wanna live in a country whereby when I go to vote it's not to ensure the other is kept out
I wanna live in a country where residents show a spirit of generosity and bands break bread with residents

I wanna live in a country where politicians do not use political safeguards designed for all as merely a safeguard for themselves
I wanna live in a country where my efforts to uphold the rights of others is not made to look wasted by the actions of those who shout loudly and stamp hardest
I wanna live in a country that doesn't always have to go to the edge so as to remind itself how far the drop is

I wanna live in a country that prides itself on its identity and heritage but not so much that there is no longer anything to be proud of
I wanna live in a country that is not defined by the colours of flags but by the colours of the rainbow
I wanna live in a country that moves beyond deals, pacts and party line to one that is moved by accommodation, kindness and compassion
I wanna live in a country that where you choose to walk is generated by curiosity and adventure rather than by fear and insecurity

I wanna live in a country where my decisions are reached rather than policed
I wanna live in a country where vision is a journey in the same direction and not a crossroads blinded by indecision
I wanna live in a country where I don't have to get into bed with one side or the other just to have a bed to get into
I wanna live in a country where opportunity for all is not merely an opportunity free for all

I wanna live in a country where language is embraced as enriching rather than the butt of jokes or a tool to alienate
I wanna live in a country where my opinions do not equate to an unwelcome invitation late at night
I wanna live in a country where the smell of fresh air does not succumb to the scent of smoke and brimstone
I wanna live in a country that does not blur lines or fudges decisions in order to protect the intolerant and the violent

I wanna live in a country where the message we leave behind is not a legacy of confusion and ambiguity
I wanna live in a country where we do not look east or south for inspiration but we look to ourselves
I wanna live in a country that does not make excuses for one side or the other but values responsibilities and rights in equal measure
I wanna live in a country that creates a new hope and not a hope to cling to

I wanna live in a country where the love we share and whom we choose to share it with is not an excuse to label me alongside those whose depravity knows no bounds
I wanna live in a country where we don't merely explain away our past yet condemn unreservedly those who follow in our footsteps
I wanna live in a country where we don't spin, whitewash or re-write what happened but write our joint narrative together
I wanna live in a country where our acceptance of sectarianism, racism, homophobia and gender inequality becomes socially unacceptable

It's much more than that

It's much more than that, much deeper
It's about connectedness that generates feelings
It's about the sense of belonging you get when you have someone to care for
It's about that feeling you have when you just fit

It's about not straying not because you don't have the option but because the person you're with makes you wanna go home everyday
It's about being in the moment every time you sit together
It's about waking up in the morning and seeing her smile, a smile that mirrors how you feel
It's about intimacy that speaks to you when words are unspoken

It's about being in separate places yet you just know your thoughts stray to one another
It's about being able to be honest in such a way that the difficult thoughts only serve to draw you closer
It's about offering reassurance in moments of doubt when it's easier to give into anger
It's about just sitting listening when your only desire is to defend yourself

It's about not merely bringing your own hopes & dreams to the table but building hopes and dreams together
It's about stopping mid conversation and turning to her and tell her one more time that you love her
It's about stopping what you're doing and walking over to her and hugging her for no other reason that you just want her to know
It's about losing yourself where you held back before and letting go and creating new boundaries

It's about turning new pages and writing new chapters of your story together
It's about spontaneously getting up and going out without stopping to think about it or just sitting in when an invite from friends await you
It's about jumping in the car and dropping everything to be with her
It's about slowing everything down and consciously savouring every moment you have together

It's about asking questions so you can begin to really know and understand better
It's about asking her to explain not to justify
It's about being true to yourself from the beginning so that you don't have to lie afterwards
It's about making good on your promises and being a man of your word

It's about a text to say you're thinking about her or a phone call out of the blue
It's about enjoying each day as it comes but not assuming there will be another day followed by another day followed by another day
It's about standing with her when she wants the ground to open up
It's about taking her hand and whispering in her ear it's going to be ok

It's about not forgetting when you started out, what brought you together, the first kiss, the images that stay in your mind more so than the rest, the things that got you through the tough times, the times your heart skipped, the moments you breathed harder and the feeling you got when you told her you loved her and she told you the same....that's what it's all about

In No Particular Order 50

I sit on the sidelines

I sit on the sidelines and one by one I watch them come together
A smile here
A touch there
Undiluted happiness knows no limitation

A gift to each other they share moments
Carefree
Unconcerned
Willing to stretch further than they have for some time

Clearly in the throes of new love or a love that has endured there is a natural flow
Bound by a heightened sense of care for one another
Every decision is collaboration
Every thought is not independent but a defiant act of unity

They find their place
Somewhere they can be alone
Somewhere they can be one
Somewhere they can milk privacy and precious moments together

Unconcerned about those around them
Unmoved by others who perhaps catch every third word
Others who sit alone wishing they could share something similar
They indulge fantasy

They sip from their cups
Listening intently as the latest chapters converge
Broken only by gasps or laughter, the call of staff or the cry of a young child
They continue, their eyes smitten, hands clasped in one another

Time passes
There is no time, only this moment
A moment capturing their sense of one another
Joy, kindness, care, compassion, a love that exudes plentiful

A love that is neither contrived nor manufactured
A love that seeks solace in each other
A love that burns, that nurtures, that excites
A love that consumes, that bleeds, that courses slowly through the veins

They emerge, they stop, they look around
They gather their thoughts, their things, themselves
They rise, they stand, they look to one another
As if there might not be another moment

They know the gap will be short
They follow the same path, bidding farewell to no-one
They leave the present, the past, envy, joy and serenity in their wake
I still sit on the sidelines

Who am I kidding?

Who am I kidding trying to be brave
Pretending it doesn't hurt
Doing the right thing and saying nothing
Wanting not to be seen as something I'm not

I wear my heart on my sleeve
Can't help it, it's in my DNA
The desire to speak out
A culture that taught me to keep schtum

I can't do that, I just can't
I can't sit idly by and pretend
This is killing me
The do nothing approach that honours the wishes of others making it easy for them

What about me?
What about how I feel?
Why am I holding back?
I want to scream but not on the inside

I need to bleed, to feel, to breathe
I need to share, to express, to cry
I need to be heard, to escape, to shout
I need to be held, to be hugged, to be safe

I know we're both feeling it
I know we wonder, we think, we debate, we contemplate, we want to, we don't
I know we need the sound of our voices
I know we can't go from intensity to silence seamlessly

It's as unnatural as it is strategic
It's as empty as it is safe
It's as unwanted as it is needed
It's as painful as it is necessary

Silence is golden yet it is bronze
It is therapeutic yet it invades
It is welcome yet it is uninvited
It is reassuring yet it is unnerving

Let it out but to whom
Don't keep it to yourself they say but who to share it with?
Sharing is caring but who really cares
Get it off your chest but all I wanna do is beat mine

Who the hell am I kidding?

Austerity

Austerity, not so long ago a word I never knew
Oh how it has consumed us, how we have embraced it
As if it was always there, waiting to be welcomed back into the fold
Patiently waiting for its 15 minutes to say, I told you so

It means what exactly?
From where did it emerge?
We know it, we can sense it, we live it, we see it
How did it creep up on us like it did?

A small word, an impressive word, almost likeable
Seems irrelevant yet conveys immense power
Holds us to ransom, dictates government policy
Demonises the weak and the vulnerable

Poisons minds, galvanises ideology, holds court
Pits neighbour against neighbour
Provides the righteous with ammunition
Provide the meek with desolation

Widens the divide, deepens the sense of injustice
Nurtures and espouses mantras and calls of sharing the load
Demands selflessness yet creates animosity
Reinforces and embeds deceit

It does not lend itself to the weak
If you have nothing you can't trim, reduce, cut back, go without
It doesn't cost the wealthy a thought
Why would it if you haven't had to go without, to choose between, to prioritise, to sacrifice,
to dash expectation, to give up on a dream

Austerity, a word unlike any other, it occupies the battle for hearts and minds
Perpetrates myths and redefines reality
Colonises hopelessness, sanitises debate, eats away at our ethical boundaries
Convinces us that it's the only way

Who's in control? The same people pre-austerity
The guys who led us here
The guys who convinced us to share their values, their beliefs, their ideals
The same guys who ask us to share in austerity

I don't need...

I don't need the flash car because a modest one will still get me to B
I don't need the big house because I can only sit in one room at a time
I don't need the gym because I have nothing to prove
I don't need the vast wealth because it's of no use to me when I'm gone

I don't need the god because I can't see my soul when I'm alive so how will I know what it looks like when I can no longer breathe
I don't need the second home in the sun just to get away from it all
I don't need all the new technology because it means feeling downgrade when you don't upgrade
I don't need the plush hotel as I will spend so little time in it

I don't need first class, priority or speedy boarding because we'll all still land at the same time
I don't need drugs as I don't seek to escape
I don't need any political ideology because I don't want to deny myself countless opportunity
I don't need bravado because I'll end up having to keep pretending

I don't need it to be always sunny because I want to appreciate when it is
I don't need to conform to one way of thinking just to discover we were all wrong
I don't need popularity when principle will remain my true friend
I don't need to be loud to reassure others that I'm still here

I don't need to need to get what I want

What a Nation the UK is

Whether it's the obsession or portrayal of those on benefits
Or the way the talentless castrate their way through X-Factor hits
Irrespective of how you measure success
Be it financiers, economists or bankers tips
Oh what a nation the UK is

Be it the immigrant, the asylum seeker or the casual refugee
Scared witless of them all is the feeble you and me
Embroiled in scandals, cover-ups or dirty deeds
Be it politicians, celebrity or the judiciary
Oh what a nation the UK is

Battle hardened with the sins of the past
Be it collusion, Iraq or the Ghurkhas wrath
Dedicated to the values of justice and equality
White-wash Hillsborough, Stephen Lawrence and history
Oh what a nation the UK is

Ignore the failures towards children, the young and the elderly
Campaign against a Human Rights Bill you decree
Choose a future made up of the holy three
Business, banking and the economy
Oh what a nation the UK is

The Humble Politician

Ah the humble politician
Able to dodge eggs, flour, bullets and accusations
But never known to duck an argument, an invitation to a party or an expenses claim

A hearty soul
Bears the brunt of criticism, ridicule, cynicism and misinterpreted sound bites
Has the ability to do his job without supervision, doesn't need a licence to practice, requires no qualifications and his word is without recourse

A principled individual
Privileged and honoured to represent his constituents, the interests of her party, the wishes of their community and the aspirations of society
And duly rewarded with more than twice the average salary, running costs to cover expenses you and I can only dream about and doesn't have to complete time sheets

A committed soul
Shuns the limelight, gets on with the task in hand, loathes publicity-seeking persona's and would rather burn the midnight oil
Will if duty requires represent the party on various public bodies and committees, appear on radio and television to defend the party line, will attend functions, events and dinners to ensure the party is visible and will show balls of steel under a public onslaught by fielding questions they have no knowledge of, insight into and ability to convince us of the answer too

A brave fighter
In the face of adversity, at the edge of reason, in the eye of the storm and in the valley of death
Can find in his darkest hour the ability to reach out to those in his community and not to those who he needs to, can stand together as one with those in positions of influence and power, is able to articulate in a dynamic manner his values and ethics without any hint of arrogance, can easily clarify comments further so as to avoid being misinterpreted once more

Ah the humble politician....genius!

The Starbucks User

From all the Starbucks users in their various guises
To the one-drink wifi scrounger and the exhausted mother with her little surprises

From the happy couple who declare their love
To the lycra-loving gym user & her tight-fitting stuff

From the builders who skipped Mc Donalds cause they just got paid
To the balding silver-haired academic on a verbal tirade

From the starbucks fan who just likes to be seen
To the aspiring career girls who share the teenage dream

From the divorced father who treats his kids to a Mediterranean-style lunch
To the semi-retired sun-kissed primary school teachers who meet up for brunch

From the Klumps, a trail of napkins, straws, sticks, wrappers, cups and crumbs
To the quiet, introvert and lonely who sit and twiddle their thumbs

From the readers and writers who look for a quiet space
To the passing groups of visitors who take over the place

From the grandparents and grandkids who look to kill some time
To the haven't seen each other in ages and their catch up lines

From the members of staff who have no option but to go
To the police officers who seek solace in a calorie-laden espresso

From the tablet-user who makes laptop man look out of date
To the generous father who feeds his family of eight

From the David Beckham-esque young men groomed so smooth
To the muscle bound gym loving guys who have something to prove

From the professional colleagues who travel in pairs
To the motor cycle enthusiasts who can't wait to share

From the actors, musicians and producers that plan their next feat
To the coaches, fun runners and athletes who prepare for their forthcoming meet

From the students, the holiday makers and the passing trade
To the business men, business women and professionals who have made the grade

From the labourers, paramedics and all types of crew
To the secularists, the believers and the unruly few

From the minorities, the non-native speakers and those we have missed
To the visionaries, lonely chief exec's and workers feeling just a little depressed

Starbucks users, we salute you all!

Another book of poems by Fergal Barr

Three Hours from a Knock on Your Door

As night draws to a close and we both lie in bed
Thoughts turn often to things that lie ahead

Where is he now and does he still think of me?
What is she doing and what thoughts occupy she?

What would we be doing at this moment in time?
Pillow Talk perhaps as we'd lay side by side?

How will it truly be now as we emerge from the past?
What of the future and the stories we had?

In our own worlds with emotions that combined us
In our own space with feelings that now divide us

And as our bodies tire and our eyes grow weary
What might we both give right now for a few hours with thee?

And sure if I'm wrong and it's only I that thinks so
Then take this as nothing more than a text from a friend to say hello

And as sleep overcomes you and you prepare for tomorrow's chores
Remember I'm only three hours from a knock on your door

On Reflection

I have reached that point where I am now content rather than pursuing happiness - only to be disappointed - but I smile and laugh when life invites me.

I don't look for happiness in any case, I prefer to use the word contentment because the search for happiness can be endless and is always being redefined in many ways.

I truly live in each moment (or as much as I can) but without living it as if it were going to be the last because I know not when the last moment will visit and thus I should embrace the gift of time.

I endeavour to give a lot knowing that it cannot always be the best for some yet I wish them well as they journey through expectation.

I am eternally grateful for the many opportunities that have presented themselves in many guises yet know and acknowledge that luck and coincidence lends a hand.

I will look back upon my many achievements and moments of pride but I am humbled by those whose grace and integrity never sought the limelight.

I will look back upon all that I have accomplished and will remember those who have helped me to secure those accomplishments.

I will no longer focus my energies on others to the extent that I have but rather give my energies to a more noble cause, one whereby I concentrate on merely pursuing a simple existence and endeavour to care that I live a life of care and compassion.

In a world where the many human values we cherish are often belittled and watered down there is really a lot I cannot influence nor control yet I can live my life in a way that is about committing to caring, acts of compassion and love and doing so this can be my message.

Failing Forwards

Failing forwards, Failing backwards
Failing sideways, Failing with courage

Failing this, Failing that
Failing honestly, Failing to chat

Failing alone, Failing with friends
Failing to notice, Failing to comprehend

Failing inside, Failing outside
Failing gloriously, Failing with pride

Failing you, Failing me
Failing us all, Failing to see

Failing to think, Failing to stop
Failing to answer, Failing at the top

Failing to acknowledge, Failing to perceive
Failing to laugh, Failing to breathe

Failing to be original, Failing to create
Failing to hope, Failing to be great

Failing in an instant, Failing over time
Failing in a heartbeat, Failing in my mind

Failing to hope, Failing to believe
Failing is not despair but a distant memory

There is always room for failure

Websites – the stuff of legends

Google - to look for stuff

Bing – to look for stuff also but just not as popular or as good as Google

E-Bay – to sell stuff you don't need or want

Couch Surfing – to find somewhere to get away from your stuff

Facebook - to keep in touch with people about stuff or to let people know what stuff you've got going on

Twitter – to let people know you give a stuff about stuff

E-mail – to send stuff

Royal mail – to send stuff slowly

Moodle – setting up dates so you can organise stuff

Instagram – post photos about stuff

Viber – free phone calls about stuff

Snapchat – when you have instantly forgettable stuff to chat about

Vimeo – to show short videos about stuff

YouTube – when you want to make fun of stuff

Amazon – when you want to order stuff

Old friends reunited – stuff you don't want to talk about

Sound Cloud – other people can hear your stuff whilst not being in your company just in case your stuff is naff

Apps – TMS: Too Much Stuff

The Facebook User

'The Activist' – the person who promotes campaigns, fights injustice and highlights inequality

'The Observationalist' – the person who share things for amusement

'The Commentator' – Troll by another name

'The Reporter' – the person who invites you into their household and shares details of what's going on in their life assuming that we're interested

'The Lonely' – the person who tells you everything they do, where they are and what they eat

'The Extended Family Person' – the person who treats Facebook like their family, i.e., 'good morning Facebook, good night Facebook'

'The Ideologist' – the person who constantly references God and attributes all happiness to him or her and their plan for us all

'The Liker' – the person who 'likes' your stuff even if it makes no sense or means nothing to them

Heart Stopping

Just for a moment you really do pause
Emotions free, you look into their eyes
You have no answer, you can't find words
You think of nothing else, you hold your breath

Your cover your mouth, you are touched
You are truly human, you are humble
You can breathe, you can't breathe
You can imagine but you can't imagine

You see beauty but it's lost to the world, you see life but it's gone
You see energy and vitality but it's ashes, you feel pain but you're so far away
You see humility and humanity but you really have no idea.....
You want to feel but you feel false

You bottle it up and try to do something different
You want to create change but life will go back to normal
You are human, you are breathing
You are lucky, remember you are lucky

I am lucky, we are lucky
For the grace of whatever go we
Luck, just luck
Born in this place, born in this land

Free to wander, free to decide
Free to laugh, to sing, to dance
But not really free, not free when slaughter is common place, when our masters that we elected paved the way, and only the few who opposed were drowned out, muffled, ridiculed, ostracised, labelled

Truly Heart Stopping

Struggling

I'm really struggling, really struggling
I thought she was the one, I still believe it
Everything points in this direction
Except the most important aspect, she

Right now I'm just getting by
No job or tasks to occupy me
The void is immense
The gap she has left knows no bounds

I sit alone, my thoughts for company
And when I move to be with others
I merely drift among them
Tears held back by my own pride

I could choose to celebrate what we shared
But the sense of loss overcomes me
There'll be better days ahead of course
But right now it feels it's not possible

Inisheer

Peace, solitude, serenity
The hum of the engine
The clitter-clatter of conversation
A gentle rocking side to side
Cool spray soothes a warm surface
Birds stopping only to sail alongside
Hazy sunshine melts into the horizon
Strong breeze greets our every gesture
Waves cut without care never to be replaced
A steady hand guides us forward
A stop en route as smiles and steps aboard are exchanged
Jumping onto land with decisions to consider
Left or right both will join each other later
Go with the flow and let destiny guide us
A road to seemingly nowhere take us to the edge of our imagination
Postcard scenery awaits our curiosity
A left here, a right there, a straight on at the next
A turn off there, a turn off here, a jump over that, a leap over this
An exploration of coastline of a million twists and turns
A rugged bishbosh mishmash of millennia carved out by repeat wave offenders
A rusting hulk befitting the story bestowed upon us by three craggy priests
A dander along windy roads as we pass on the horse driven taxis
A return to civilisation where voices, drinks, food, smell and sunshine collide
A boat to catch and waves to fix
Land greets us again with memories savoured forever

Galway

The world passes me by now
A sudden mass of culpability shared by all around me
The glitter of conversations lighten up a mouldy discourse
A diverse and humble landscape surrounds her natives
A child chases a bird whilst others adorn parents arms as gifts from another place
Intentions released in a hubbub of chatter
Business continues as a cacophony of white noise
A stirring restlessness as an exchange of vows convenes movements in countless directions
Defined by shapes, colours, style, sound, posture to the discerning eye
A multitude of notions, ideas, views, thoughts nurture a bubble of culture
An endemic plague of difference greets every corner, every juncture, and every possibility
An identity no longer defined by history or conviction but wrapped in a blanket of newness, every thread and stitch woven together by destiny, need, desire and celebration
A pulse shared by all with each beat of a common heart echoing to the footsteps that never cease no matter the hour, no matter the day, no matter the occasion
Vibrancy abounds in an eclectic fashion as it seduces every soul in a river of courage
and aspiration
Desire, belief and a will to be part of something greater than the sum of its parts
A feeling that ignites with every step you take
The shore bends and gathers momentum as cafes and galleries conjure up moments of euphoria
Not enormous, not big, compactness unites its people, its stories, its crave for something more
It doesn't have to pretend, it is, it has always been, it feels it, it lives it, the people know
This is a place to be, this is a place like no other
It is Galway

A Single Heart

A trembling inside, a feeling of excitement
Unable to eat, pressing hard on the table
She looks for an exit

Concentration at a loss, anguish at the moments passing
She digs for courage, engaging her desires
Her eyes scan people and place

With just a little doubt, and a moment's hesitation
She stands tall, walking the short distance to uncertainty
She focuses on her task

Grasping at reasons, trumpeting single stories
The journey underway, a medium for discourse
She eyes a seat close by

Settling at his side, a moment in time beckons her
Uncertainty craves attention
She savours the adrenalin fuelled pause

Words trickle but with little coherence
A bumbling idiot she thinks
Charming and endearing he imagines

Content is not important as gesture is rewarded
He responds in kind destined to fuel the bumbling
Discourse slowly takes over

Trying not to confer status upon one another
They slowly breathe
Wondering of one another who is one another

An invitation to continue nurtures excitement
Thoughts turn to possibilities
A process of discovery creates opportunity

Moments become stretched and time doesn't curate
Gestures from a place of compassion consume
Life can do its own carefree thing

She hopes that he hopes as he hopes that she hopes
A journey of bends and twists, dreams and fantasies
Perhaps a single heart no more

Joe

Joe either stayed in his room
Or sat in the corner of the hall way
Why they ever brought him I just don't understand

He'd always ask me for a cigarette
Yet telling me how bad they were
Why they ever brought him I just don't know

His grey suit tattered and dirty
His voice rough and his walk stooped
Why they ever brought him I just can't tell

A man of wit if not idle chit-chat
He looked for ways to escape everyday monotony
Why they every brought him in I'm sure it was a mistake

A throw-back to another era
He'd embellish stories to delight a forgetful audience
Why they every brought him in I'm sure they forgot themselves

Still in control....for now
Yet destiny beyond his control
Why they every brought him in shames us

A light in a mansion of dim hallways
His hope burns bright but despair brighter
Why they every brought him in placates those who go home at five

A commitment to make the most of it
His eyes swollen from tender moments alone
Why they every brought him in escapes logic

A decision he does not question
He is left pondering who he was and what he has become
Why they every brought him in is policy at its worst

A man robbed of his dignity
Independence that took flight at the stroke of someone's pen
Why they every brought him in is unforgiveable

Joe, his name is Joe
Undeserving of his grotty suit, in this grotty room in a home of impending death
Why they every brought him in served no-one but only that someone who never came to visit him

My Garden

The street light beckons the trees as they stand monster-like in the dark
A minimal breeze forces no leaf to stray as only the noise of a passing car gives life to the moment
The stars in the sky hazy only by a veil of cloud as it battles to keep out the inevitable
A sip of red soothing against the beauty of musical therapy
Memories invoked as this long awaited moment nestles gently under me
I am bliss, I am peace, I am thoughtful, I am serenity
A garden as natural as the day it was deserted
Left to fend for itself as only it can
A garden of wild unadulterated carelessness
A garden of unwanted clashing with the neighbours carefully caressed harmony
This is my garden, a garden of supreme unwritten rules
A garden that pokes its friends in the eye and its enemies with two fingers
A garden that is unrivalled by competition and cares not for the time
A garden that is supreme, confident in itself and first in a competition of one
This is the most certainly not a marks and sparks garden
It is truly mine, truly unblemished, truly unruly, truly uncared for, true to itself
This is my garden warts 'n' all

Picture Yourself

Picture yourself on a hospital bed
About to be sold for the hair on your head
Cut backs, knock backs and all that goes with it
Steady complaints as the waiting list grows

Pity yourself coz it don't get much better
A cold sombre day and some turbulent weather
Depleted resources, lack of funding
Cancelled operations, staff shortages mounting

Punish yourself as it becomes the norm
A place of salvation laced with scorn
Threatened strikes and acts of defiance
Seven-day mantras and oversubscribed service

Brace yourself as you try to stay alive
Check your postcode as the lottery decide
Hope you're submitted by the end of the week
Or dig out your will and give it a tweak

Prepare yourself as you're due to go in
Wait for notice of your cancellation
Hope grows shorter with each gasp you wheeze
Find a service crumbling brought to its knees

Remind yourself you were around to see it begin
Cite stories of marching to save its very skin
Look all around you noting what you see
Stay true to the notion of a service that should be free

Arm yourself to the teeth with fortitude and desire
Hold true to the beliefs we once shared and aspired
Do not let the criminals plunder it to an unforgiveable death
Save this piece of heritage with every dying breath

Pleasing Others - Part II

I spent my entire childhood being told what to do
I spent my entire adolescence being convinced about what I could have
I spent my entire adulthood being persuaded about what I should get
And now I will spend my entire later years worrying about how to get it back

I spent jobs meeting the targets of others
I spent days waiting for the arrival of moments
I spend time dressing it up for someone who is no-one in particular
And now I spend time reflecting why

I spent time honouring the absence of those who did not show
I spent time composing the words to soften the blow of those who stamp their feet
I spent time committed to effort only to watch the effortless prevail
And now I spend moments considering its worth

I spent a fortune investing in a plan for old age
I spent an entirety nurturing beliefs that seem to betray me
I spent a lifetime trying to be someone for everyone only to be judged
And now I spend days pondering its value

I spent days pursuing ideals constructed by others with invisible motivation
I spent months planning catch-up in a reality dictated by others without compassion
I spent years trying to get there only to arrive at the dawn of 'it doesn't really matter anyway'
And now, well now, now I have stopped, I am content, pleasing others no-more

Saving Grace

Laughter, music and children are my saving grace
They're my escapism in times of stress
They're my kitsch in the fashion of odd
They're my wholesale changes in a life of same

Laughter, music and children are my saving grace
They're my honour in times of embattlement
They're my tears when I have none left to give
They're my undressing in a world masked by pain

Laughter, music and children are my saving grace
They're my intention when the world has lost its
They're my endeavours when I don't feel the upstanding citizen
They're my saving grace when I have nothing left to give

Laughter, music and children are my saving grace
They're my light in my darkest moment
They're my reason for not letting go
They're my smile when it has deserted me

Laughter, music and children are my saving grace
They're my moment when time stands still
They're my very essence when I can see it no longer
They're my being when touch no longer feels

Laughter, music and children are my saving grace
They're my heart when it plays the strings
They're my mind when imagination wanders
They're my playfulness in a world of serious

Laughter, music and children are my saving grace
They're my heartbeat when my pulse fades
They're my destiny when the road splits
They're my defence in a court of law

Laughter, music and children are my saving grace
They're my defiance when all seems lost
They're my eyesight when blindsided
They're my soul when I shall breathe no more

There's not a day

There's not a day that passes when you don't occupy my thoughts
There's barely an hour that goes by when you don't cross my mind
There's rarely an evening that arrives when I don't speak with you
There's not a sound of an engine pulling up that I don't wish was yours
There's not many nights that draw to a close when I wish you weren't close
There's hardly a morning I awake when I don't imagine your face next to mine
There's rarely a day that passes when my body does not crave yours
There's not many songs I hear that the lyrics don't whisper your name
There's not many memories that don't lead to you
There's not many a journey that don't start out the same
And there's not many a day when I still don't follow the dream

Encore no more

Five years today an angel appeared to me from on high
As if by virtue of a stairway to the stars carved from stone
An image etched in my mind
I can summon it as if only it were yesterday
How she stood, the colour of her coat, the bend of her figure
Her hair shining darkly, draping her shoulders
She held me from that moment
Something stirred, a space clearing
Clarity grappling with confusion
Emotions triggered, a light flickering in the distance
My own mind foggy with little sobriety
But memory rallied, a forget me not colouring my conscience
It hunted me down, captured my imagination
Allowed me to think the possible, create the probable
But never beset me with doubt, how to grow a future I do not know
Just ask her, just go for it, let her know
Akin to a scene from a film, but this is real life
Enough info to create interest, enough to be found, enough to begin a conversation
Against a background of wet and miserable
The cold air broken by the warmth of intention
An unspoken promise to speak again
A belief nurtured in an unknown outcome
Nervous energy animating a sense of destiny
Dormant feelings awoken by tenderness and care
A journey ahead with destiny written all over it
Bumps in the road but love is the destination
Exploration of unchartered discoveries navigate incoming
Driven by fate, belonging, allure, passion, love, joy, laughter, desire, commitment, belief, destiny, admiration, care, daring, hope, it was all that it could be but not all that it could have been
We took our places in line, at the front and we bowed, curtseyed, bowed again, curtseyed once more, many times, until we left the stage by separate doors, with memories, love and destiny applauding loudly and willing us to return for an encore
The music faded, the curtains dropped, the audience exited, the props put away, ropes tied up, ushers clearing a path, lights dimmed, signs carefully removed and doors easing gently to a state of neutrality

Encore no more….but not never…..

How do I say I Love You on this special day?

How do I say I Love You on this special day?
Is it the dinner we can't afford that waits until we get paid?
Is it the flowers by pre-order that lack a certain care?
Or is it the desire to be with you across a passionate stare?

How do I say I Love You on this special day?
Is it a romantic walk across a specially selected Galway moonlit bay?
Is it an overwhelming gift all style yet no substance?
Or is it the sleepy hand cream moments that number in their hundreds?

How do I say I Love You on this special day?
Is it a mere reprinted card that is no more than a charade?
Is it a louder than words gesture for the public domain?
Or is it simply an arm around your shoulder when you are in pain?

How do I say I Love You on this special day?
Is it an over priced, over packaged and over the top display?
Is it a larger than life social media post to placate a sense of doubt?
Or is it overcoming the difficulties that make you wanna shout?

How do I say I Love You on this special day?
Is it the handcrafted chocolates in their ornamental tray?
Is it the pampering gift set that makes you feel more you?
Or is it the unrelenting commitment to see this thing through?

How do I say I Love You on this special day?
Is it the pomp and circumstance in another way?
Is it the specially commissioned voucher where you get to choose?
Or is it the promise to listen carefully and walk a mile in your shoes?

How do I say I Love You on this special day?
Is it the special valentine moment you expect but dare not say?
Is it the surprise trip to somewhere we have not been?
Or is it creating a future together no one else has seen?

I can't escape you

I can't escape you
I love and hate it in equal measure, it keeps me alive, it keeps me feeling, it reassures me I am more than an empty shell
Every day my body has a physical reaction to you
I hear a song, a new one, an old one, I live a memory, I see an image, I walk the same footsteps, I travel the same road
I don't tell you, it means something, heart breaking, gut wrenching, steals a breath, almost out of body experience, but it won't change anything, I can only live it through memory
It takes me back, takes me there, relives that moment, grabs my every fibre
A realisation that I'm still bound to those feelings, not just sentiment, but they are deep, enshrined, embedded, lived, present, with each breath, uncompromising
It's incredible, almost a year, and I feel it's as if it's yesterday
I don't want a new scenario, I want a new scenario
I can't escape it, I don't want to, I don't want to try, I want to, I need to
The picture on the mantelpiece, to remind me, what I had, what I lost, to remind me what I have done so I can be punished for the damage I have caused, a reminder, maybe always, perhaps till I have let go, till I can truly let go, or this feeling of yesterday becomes a distant tomorrow
I don't write, I don't call, I didn't, because I'm powerless to change things, I had no reason to believe I could
I feel, I don't feel, I'm not allowed to feel, my feelings are not allowed, they have no legitimacy, I feel no more, feel only pain, feel nothing, feels easier to feel nothing, to become that empty shell, empty shells can do no damage

Old Man

Old Man
Sways to the sound of an imaginary soundtrack
Recalls days of a leaner existence
Taps out a monologue only he can understand

Melodies bind together a diverse audience
Voices charm unspoken expectation
Perspiration rises like the notes on his page
Cameras capture future forgotten stories

Old Man
Barely able to distinguish reality
Laments yester-deals of tomorrow
Unable to conceal his pain

Harmonies ignite impatient emotion
Choruses etched across young faces
Guitar solos in everyone's hands
Countless encores only a request away

Old Man
Harbours glory still yet barely knows what day it is
Convinced the call is gonna come
Waiting for opportunity to sound a knock on his door

Long play, short play, extra play, radio play
Interviews, articles, release dates, tour venues
Concerts, gigs, intermissions, studio recordings
Signings, pictures, promotions, parties

Old Man
The knock arrives
A gentle reminder that it's time
Same time next week, if he indeed remembers

Why do people do what they do?

Challenges and changes affecting our evolution and some refuse to take account
Challenges we face but we stand idly by
Challenging ourselves to keep learning but refusing to do so
Change we know that is coming but we are too busy to consider
Creativity we don't conspire with to make the necessary difference
Economies that serves only the invisible hand
Finance that counts on our every move but we cannot count upon
Future that is in front of us but won't be there
Our brain that is the envy of the universe but we know so little about
Humour we seem to be losing slowly
Inequality that shows no sign of abating
Knowing how our mind works but assuming it works in our favour only
Knowing the reality but we choose to ignore it
Leadership we need but we fear it
Life's important questions we don't ask
Mindset we seem indebted too
Modern health disorders we have promoted to new levels
New thinking we choose to turn away from
Our approach that makes no sense
Perception we are stuck with
Personalities we won't abandon
Perspective we never revise
Politics we are hamstrung by
Product of our ancestors but they left the scene
Religion that eternally competes
Scientific minds that are not fixed but fixed minds that are not scientific
Social interaction that is more social construct
Things we need to deal with but just a minute…..
Thinking that is either/or, this or that or black and white
We are who we are and we are where we are because…..we are…..
Because this is why people do what they do

The place, it was a-jumping

The place, it was a-jumping
The glass was half full
The ladies were too
It was just like a scene from that Caffrey's ad
You know the one
When the Irish lads were all thinking of home

The place, it was a-jumping
The bar was rocking
Everyone waiting their turn
To and fro
Foot rails laughing
When the Irish lads were telling that story once more

The place, it was a-jumping
The right mixture of parlour music
Easy listening
You know the kind
The kind that pushes your buttons
When the Irish lads sang along but didn't know the words

The place, it was a-jumping
A hive of activity
None of it makes any sense
But it's all perfectly co-ordinated
The sort that just makes you stop to watch
When the Irish lads were starting to hug

The place, it was a-jumping
An owners dream come true
All cooped up with no place to go
The swaying and harmonies commence
You know the way
When the Irish lads are nearing completion

The place, it was a-jumping
All a gathering in the middle
United in song, protest and lament
The hugs, the promises, the falling over....together
A moment that can never be created again
When the Irish lads had only home to go to

The Resignation Poem

I tried to be present, visible, warm, friendly and genuinely interested
You're 'too casual'
I tried to be pragmatic, build consensus, seek thoughts and opinions
They 'should fear you'
I tried to initiate, to lead, to create, to be pro-active
'Don't change it, keep it as it is'
I tried to make time for conversation, ask questions, collate information and paint a picture
'That's not your responsibility'
I tried to be me
'Stop being a youth worker'
I tried to get to know the area, its dynamic, the work that goes on, its key players and build alliances
'Stop going to meetings'
I tried to recoup my losses
'You're not allowed'
I tried to fix a situation of their making
'Let me think how to deal with this'
I decided it was time to go
'You're making the right decision'
I made it easy for them
'You can go now'

Sacked and Dumped in a week

Sacked and Dumped in a week
Not your typical seven days
Not something everyone can say
A joke that went awry
Messages taken out of context

Sacked and Dumped in a week
Never saw that coming
Cardiac material
Attacked on both fronts
Double Whammy!

Sacked and Dumped in a week
A jolt if there ever was one
Just about digesting the first
Boom! A second comes along
Very lonely place

Sacked and Dumped in a week
Out of leftfield
Heartbroken and numb
Empty and desolate
Abandoned

Sacked and Dumped in a week
How did it get to this?
Where has reason gone?
Whatever happened to context?
Is this the reality we live in now?

Sacked and Dumped in a week
A test of resolve
No option but to survive
The pain will subside
Think, not feel

Sacked and Dumped in a week
You're on your own now
Rely on no-one
Trust only you
Make your own luck

Sacked and Dumped in a week
It is what it is
Tomorrow is a new day
Not the first
I won't be the last

50 Years, 50 Lessons

1. Rarely is anything as it appears
2. Very little in life is certain
3. There is never just one answer
4. There are no silver bullets
5. It's too easy to say people are dumb, there's always a reason
6. Daydreaming is good
7. Good behaviours are contagious
8. Too much information is a bad thing
9. Social media isn't journalism
10. Don't deal with the what should be's, deal with the what is's
11. Your beliefs are your behaviour
12. Before you condemn ask what would you have done
13. Have at least one mantra
14. One weekend per year with friends
15. One activity per week for only you
16. Never go to a party you're not invited too
17. Be sure of your values
18. Nothing is fixed, much is random
19. Technology is a tool, not a way of life
20. If you don't know, you don't know
21. Develop your own ideological statement to help steer you
22. Decide how you are going to be heard
23. Laugh, and laugh time and time again
24. Don't deal in absolutes
25. Do it because you are willing, don't expect anything in return
26. Nobody owes you anything
27. You have to make your own luck
28. Happiness is elusive, contentment is within reach
29. People need not have to change, it's your expectations that do
30. The word 'should' is of no use to anyone
31. Perspective is the eyes in the back of your head
32. Context is everything
33. Advice should start with 'what might be useful is…'
34. Articulate your needs, not your wants
35. Know the music that is important in your life and listen to it
36. The more I know the more I realise I don't know.....really
37. Don't ask questions you might not like the answers too
38. Be honest with yourself and you can be honest with everyone
39. Ask specific questions
40. There is a difference between right and correct
41. People will say what they want to say anyway so choose your battles
42. Don't do anything that will come back to haunt you
43. People are the sum of their parts
44. Take risks but only calculated risks
45. Deal with individual issues, don't wait until they accumlate
46. There's always somebody worse off than you
47. Humour is the shortest distance between people
48. Feelings do not equal truth
49. If you have an issue with someone start with a question, not an accusation
50. There is a risk in all that you do

In No Particular Order 82

In No Particular Order

Another book of poems by Fergal Barr

Lightning Source UK Ltd.
Milton Keynes UK
UKHW010135090223
416726UK00007B/47